WENSLEYDALE & THE URE

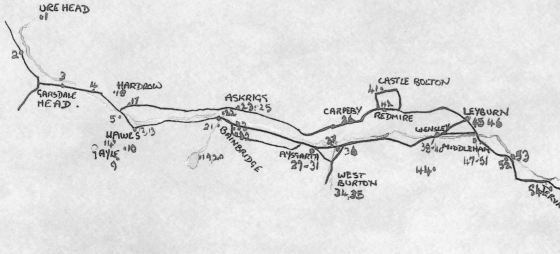

N
↑

5 MILES
APPROX

I have visited this area on and off since childhood.
Regular weekend camping expeditions as a child often
brought us to Wensleydale. As a young teacher, Ripon
was just far enough from Wakefield for a break in the
caravan with my own family. When I started working full
time as an artist we came to live in Ripon. Now Dorothy
and I explore in style from our own front door with our
25th Wedding Anniversary gift to each other – 'Harriet'.

She is a 1979 Jubilee model MGB Roadster who spent
most of her formative years in California, being brought
back to England in the 1990's. She was originally black
and gold but was resprayed in Pewter long before we met.
So glad, we would never want to change her. Black bumpers
and silver paintwork do it for us!

The River Ure begins its life high up in the Pennines at Ure Head within shouting distance of the River Eden only 100 Metres away, this river flowing west to the Irish Sea and the Ure making its way east, the story of this book. The trickle of gathering raindrops soon cut a course through the peaty upland searching for lower ground.

That might sound romantic but the driving horizontal rain we can see here means 'Top up' for Harriet, a rare occurrence unless absolutely necessary! And this is Summer! This can be an unforgiving and inhospitable place at times, not to be taken for granted, but no rain, no Ure, no Wensleydale.

It is not long before the waters become recognisable as a river, running through the gentle slopes of the upper dale. The river is flanked by stone walls dividing the fields and young lambs playing mischievously as if the world will never change. They will not be around too long though. Farming is a business and not just for us to "ooh and aah", it will be less than a year before they are off to market. Better not to think of that though. What a place to be brought up, spending time roaming free over the Yorkshire Fells.

3.

The farmers do have help of course. The graceful lines of a highly trained, fit and healthy sheepdog working in partnership with their master are an impressive sight. They cover miles of fell in a days work making light work of walls, ditches, responding instantly to waves and whistles – most of the time!

4.

5.

Appersett, illustrated here, reveals one of the many ways to enjoy the sights, sounds and smells of the countryside. A stile and finger post lead to adventure on foot wherever you go in the dale. Whether it is your wish to bag miles or just to stray a few metres from the main road, the myriad of connected footpaths offer birdsong, floral delights and a gently moving panorama. Round every corner and over every rise, a new and exciting vista opens out before you.

Don't forget though to see what is so near, the micro world within the walling stone or between the grasses. Time has a hand in the beauty too, developing the kaleidoscope of gentle colour and texture. Whatever your excuse to be here just enjoy!

Pretty soon any stream, in this case Gayle Beck, finds its way downhill to join the main river. Man has tamed the route to a point, Gayle mill being operative since 1784 as a cotton-spinning mill, later flax and then wool. By 1878 it changed to a sawmill and since renovation in recent years is a working attraction, well worth a visit.

9.

11.

10.

12.

The beck continues its journey downhill to Hawes. One of my delights is to stand on the bridge admiring the trickling stream as it tumbles over the rocky ledges, the quieter pools reflecting the tranquil scenery. Not such a delight for me though when the stream is in a mood. It soon becomes an awesome and distinctly fearful sight, the thundering torrent hurtling towards you lurching over those same stone ledges, only to dash beneath the strong stone bridge onwards and away. I do admire the skills of the bridge builders.

A vintage bus links Hawes with the Wensleydale railway which terminates at Redmire station a little way down the road. Thank goodness for nostalgia, and thanks too to the mechanics, drivers and other enthusiasts, who's limitless time keeps these bits of our history alive.

13.

14.

15.

Still in Hawes we come to the Wensleydale Creamery, happy to share their livelihood with the public. This is home to some of the finest cheese in the country – or am I biased? No Apple Pie or Christmas Cake is complete without a slice of Wensleydale cheese. This has been made even more famous by its champions 'Wallace and Gromit.' Wensleydale cheese has become a world wide phenomenon but none of it could be possible without the 'Daisy's' and 'Bluebell's' of the dale. How can you be guilty of road rage when held up by a herd wallowing along the road before milking time, udders gently swinging side to side and the gentle huff of their breath..... Ah, remember we have the top down.......

16.

17.

18.

The dale is full of wonderful places to eat and stay. One such impressive establishment is the Stonehouse Hotel, a couple of miles from Hawes. Here are offered stunning views in peaceful surroundings with excellent food and dog friendly accommodation. One previous visitor was a P.G. Woodhouse, a struggling author was near to completing his latest novel and needed a name for his principal character. Watching a local cricket match the batsmen was the Stonehouse gardener, Mr Percy Jeeves. – The rest of course, as they say, is history and a famous book was born.

A short walk or ride from here is the impressive sight of Hardraw Force which is reached through the Green Dragon Inn.

Another claim to fame is the sight of Kevin Costner having a rather cold shower beneath the fall in the film "Robin Hood Prince of Thieves". Time to reach for the video or DVD again. The area also boasts an annual band contest, a setting hard to beat, with its own stone bandstand backed by an impressive amphitheatre.

19.

Semerwater is Yorkshire's only natural lake, a result of
the retreating ice from the last Ice Age. Its windy shores
are cradled by low fells, its outlet gracefully leaving the
area beneath a fine three arch bridge before descending
with gathering vigour towards the village of Bainbridge.
This is truly one of Britain's wild places where there is
rarely more than the wind and the occasional bird cry to
disturb the tranquillity. Long may it stay this way.

20.

Here we are overlooking Bainbridge, a blanket of snow gently caressing the landscape bringing peace to the land. The area in summer sports an open green, as with many of the fine dales villages. This one is a village to negotiate on the way further up the dale but do try and take time-out here. Refreshments are available in various small cafes or try the Rose and Crown.

How many times have we passed through places like this and thought "this looks nice." Maybe a New Year resolution should be to make destinations of all those places.

The River Ure is crossed just outside the village centre by another stone multi-arched bridge. Here it is portrayed beginning to resist the rising waters derived from rain falling further up the valley.

23.

Askrigg. The church of St Oswald hosts a Christmas Tree Festival. It may be a small thing in the Great scheme of things but it epitomises the strong community spirit in many towns and villages where local action is at work. It is a pleasure for the casual visitor to call in, but the real importance in any of these activities is bringing the community together.

25.

26.

Those stonemasons have been at it again. Steps to nowhere? No, after a long journey a rider in the past would have an easy climb off or on his horse, ready to glean some refreshment from the Inn. I love to think back to slower pace of life in the the 70's in Harriet with Simon and Garfunkel emanating from the (not very period) CD player. How gentle the pace must have been when the horse ruled the road. Ok, forget the grooming, 3 day journeys and rickets............

24.

The links in Wensleydale with James Herriot, pen name of the Thirsk vet Alf Wight, intertwine fact and fiction. Many locations throughout the area were used during filming "All Creatures Great and Small", based on the story books relating his life experiences and embroidered around the many colourful characters with whom he came into contact during his working career. Here is 'Skeldale House' in Askrigg, the TV practice of the vets 'Farnon & Herriot.' In Carperby a little further down the dale is the Wheatsheaf, the honeymoon destination of Alf and his wife Joan. The commemorative plaque speaks of 'James Herriot's Honeymoon Hotel.' This is testimony to the unique story telling of Alf. We do not mind whether we are reading his fictional 'Herriot' stories or his real life. Both are equally fascinating.

27.

Further downstream the River Ure is gaining in stature and at Aysgarth it flows over layers of Limestone and shale giving rise to three areas of falls. The more well known upper falls are just upstream to a high arch bridge next to an old mill.

28.

29.

Across the road, and a short walk downstream, reveals the Middle falls. This gives a view of the parish Church of St. Andrew, but my personal favourite is the Lower Falls.

These resemble the tiers of a wedding cake and having painted them for the first time I discovered a copy of a William Turner sketch. The view he drew was almost the same some 200 years ago. As a hero of mine, it gave me goose-bumps to think of him in the same spot. It often happens. He was a prolific sketcher and certainly got around. I wonder what he would have done if somebody had invented the camera before he had his time. He would have saved a lot of wet hours in the field but we would have lost the legacy of so many sketchbooks. Go and see them if you get the chance. I like them more than his big oils. – a biased watercolourist!

Take any side road away from the through route and you can move back in time to a gentler pace of life. The tumble of buildings here in Cubeck for instance all have a purpose, I often wonder what the planning authorities might have to say about it if this was new-build!

We do need to cherish and protect our landscape with the field barns scattered randomly across a patchwork of small fields in various stages of undress as the hay harvest is made. I always am filled with wonder at the millions of man hours spent lovingly piecing the stones together to create the tracery of walling so much a part of Wensleydale. Time and the elements have a hard job to attempt to undo the effort made.

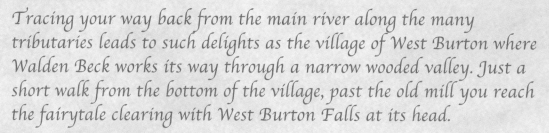

Tracing your way back from the main river along the many tributaries leads to such delights as the village of West Burton where Walden Beck works its way through a narrow wooded valley. Just a short walk from the bottom of the village, past the old mill you reach the fairytale clearing with West Burton Falls at its head.

The Village and its spectacular green is flanked by a string of sturdy stone built houses. It still supports a pub, school and shop. The striking war memorial pays tribute to the sons and daughters of the village who left his idyllic spot but never were to return. I always make a point of scanning the names in respect of their sacrifice.

34.

Having travelled through Wensleydale since I can remember I always looked for the copse of trees on the hillside as we neared Aysgarth. I have always known it as 'Lady Hill' and have watched as the trees have diminished, particularly during the storms of 1987. Under planting is ensuring the trees are there for posterity.

Less old but very nostalgic is the AA box, now a listed building. It brings back memories of the salute from patrols, that lovely yellow and silver badge (on the shelf in many a garage now I bet) and the special key. Thankfully there has been no cause to test the box this time after a good service, (thank you Mr Powell), and little bit of luck – every journey is an adventure in Harriet!

40.

38.

39.

The village of Wensley, dominated by its Church of the Holy Trinity which sadly is now no longer in regular use, has seen busier times. Hit by plague in 1563 many of the remaining villagers left for Leyburn. The building of Bolton Hall helped to rekindle expansion but the village still remains as a proud figurehead for the dale. The beautiful stone stile here is a good example of the resourceful use of durable local materials. The art of hedge-laying to rejuvenate a tired hedge is another way to harness nature to work for us, not only a stock barrier but a vital habitat for our wildlife. How about a little sales board – "Sparrow starter homes now under construction – apply within."!

41.

The dale has a fine collection of Castles and Abbeys. The Castle at Castle Bolton, completed in 1399, is still privately owned. Amongst several claims to fame Mary, Queen of Scots was imprisoned there in 1569. Now it provides a stunning view across Wensleydale – unless it happens to be raining! Often signed as Bolton Cum Redmire The larger village of Redmire once again sports one of those delightful stone stiles...... Maybe from a catalogue.......?

And now for a little escapism. The Forbidden Corner, accessed from Middleham on the Coverdale road (Ticket only), is a delightful diversion. Children are not compulsory but they do give you an excuse to be silly. Expect to get wet at times, and whilst it is safe, it can be a little scary. That just means you need to visit again when they are a bit older. Hurray!

Leyburn is one of the larger towns in the dale. The Shawl is only a few minutes walk from the centre and story goes that as Mary Queen of Scots escaped from Bolton Castle she took this route and dropped her shawl..... Now easy access for disabled allows breathtaking views of a good the dale, the road and railway cutting through the valley floor.

The Railway and town is turned over to a time gone by as the 40's weekend is enjoyed by visitor and local alike. From Home Guard to evacuees, to American GI's, and even a brown suited and bowler hatted 'Man from the Ministry' is in evidence as the weekend unfolds.

The railway stretches from Leeming to Redmire and is a super way of viewing the dale as a family treat (probably for dad anyway.)

Middleham sports another famous castle, first construction starting in 1190. In its chequered history it was used by Richard Duke of Gloucester (Soon to become King Richard III) as a base for keeping order in the north.

It is now the backdrop to much equine activity. There are a number of racehorse training stables, part of the Middleham Trainers Association, and the day is always broken by the clopping of hooves as the horses are taken out for exercise on the gallops throughout the day. If driving please take great care.

48.

47.

49.

Viewing the horses on the gallops early in the morning with a gentle mist slowly lifting is one of those satisfying sights that makes you feel nothing else matters for that moment.

Another satisfying moment though was being lucky enough to drop in on a charity 'Cream Tea Day' at the local Methodist Church. The diet starts tomorrow as the instructions given were "eat as much as you like". This is the 'Before' painting. The 'After' painting...well, I couldn't be bothered - too full!

On a wintry trip up the dale the sight of lunch time for a farmers flock tickled me. Definitely a case of 'meals on wheels'. Apologies here to the Cover Bridge Inn, just one of those ideas that never quite made it. You simply have to imagine a fine roaring fire, high back chairs and cool pint of local ale in your hand whilst choosing which fine fayre to enjoy......Well, - I suppose we are still full from the cream tea on the last page!

To stop the river feeling neglected here at Ulshaw is a serene spot where the deeper waters create a much more mirror like effect reflecting the much wider bridge needed further down the valley. This is one of those bitter sweet images for me as a watercolour artist I have in irrational fear of deep still dark water. Silly, but often good for a laugh at my expense. Even puddles beside the road on a dark night hold menace!

54.

The same scenario is evident on our roadside verges where a secret world hides from the passing motorist. Stop a while if it is safe and you can admire the rich diversity of flowers and insects making home the narrow strip of land between road and field boundary.

55.

57.

I particularly like Jervaulx Abbey as a ruin which has not been sanitised in its preservation. Flowers colonise the nooks and crannies in its crumbling walls. I admire too the love and care bestowed on each carved stone by a bygone mason.

This is a case of the sum of the parts is greater than the whole. At a distance the ruin has not got   the grandeur say of Fountains Abbey but the juxtaposition of carved stone and random vegetation creates hundreds of cameo corners to delight the artist.

56.

The area is home to an industry born out of diversification. The Moore family began their ice-cream making in Wheeton in Wharfedale in 1984, as a result of milk quotas restricting their dairy sales. Their popularity outstripped the ability to expand. The business was moved, with its herd of pedigree Guernsey cows, to High Jervaulx Farm and its continuing success is due in part I am sure to the consumption of my family!

Whether on a hot or a rainy day it is a good spot to take an afternoon trip out. Here we have grandson Russel on serious quality control duties. (I only had one to keep him company).

61.

The open space of Masham Market Place is home to several annual events in addition to a regular weekly market. The Masham steam fair is climaxed by a parade of machinery, from tractors to fairground engines, leaving the showground to gather en-masse on the square. The attack on the senses is quite something as the heavyweights attack the steep incline to the centre. One warning – don't wear white......

A little more sedate but none the less quirky is the annual Sheep Fair at the end of September which owes its origins to the huge sheep sales of bygone days. Now it is a feast of fun with everything Sheepy! Sheep races, best sheep, shearing demonstrations and lots of side shows aimed at helping raise money for local charities. Not even Foot and Mouth stopped it! Local schools were encouraged to build sheep 'scarecrows' to continue the tradition.

60.

Probably the biggest claim-to-fame in Masham is the Two Breweries. Theakston Brewery was built in 1875 but the family had been brewing since 1827 and has been in family hands for most of the time except for a spell between 1981 and 2003 when it fell under the wing of Scottish and Newcastle. Some of the Ales are sold in Oak Casks made and repaired by the cooper Jonathan Manby, one of only a few active in the country. Here Jonathan is working on one of a pair of barrels for Prince Charles' home at Highgrove.

There can be few jobs more enjoyable than working with aromatic oak in a brewery – and in Yorkshire!

64.

62.

63.

66. Equally worth a visit is the Black Sheep Brewery opened in 1992. Through the take over of Brewery by Scottish and Newcastle disenchantment led Paul Theakston to dream of independence once again. To cut a long story short he managed to acquire the old Lightfoot Brewery maltings building in Masham and by judicious searching across the country was able to assemble the present equipment, such as these slate Yorkshire squares, from a variety of sources as other breweries were 'rationalised' i.e. closed!

The installation has been completed and developed very tastefully and with the visitor in mind. This includes a very good Bistro.

Sheep and Masham are synonymous; therefore Paul wished to use Sheep as a name since the word Masham was being used by others. This was a little tame and his renegade actions, opening up as a competitor to the old family firm, probably contributed to the 'Black Sheep' trademark name being coined.

65.

67.

68.

69.

70.

70.

Back to the River and its meanderings through a beautiful wooded valley. Hackfall woods is one of the many hidden gems of the area, where glimpses of the river's ripples and pools can be caught through the trees on a narrow woodland path.

Along the route are a number of fascinating follies recently undergoing renovation. Access is from Grewelthorpe or a small car park further along the road towards Masham.

West Tanfield is probably one of the most photographed points along the River Ure. Standing in the middle of the bridge you could have had one foot in West Yorkshire and one in North Yorkshire. Boundry changes in 1974 put a stop to that. Looking upstream the well maintained gardens cradle the red roofs of the old cottages, the Church of St. Nicholas and the Marmion Tower, a C15th gatehouse to an old riverside manor house, now long gone. There is a lovely view from the tower back downstream, much admired by the many pigeons which make it their home.

This misty rural scene is just off the road back towards Ripon. I like to imagine the sheepy conversations about "how unfair is it to leave us out on this filthy cold morning."

Sheep talk in thoughts you know....... Stay with them long enough and you may will pick them up......... Baaaah!

Having Fountains Abbey on our doorstep is one of the plus points of living in Ripon. It is a great place to find yourself in any weather, in any season. Built in a secluded valley along the River Skell, it still maintains a majestic appearance telling of times of influence by the Church now long gone.

74.

This is a World Heritage Site and visited by thousands of tourists every year. They also enjoy the water gardens begun by John Aislabie in the 1720's and continued by his son William, the estate then encompassing an area from the Abbey ruins to the Valley of the Seven Bridges. An abundance of wildlife is present. The pheasants are reared for a shoot on certain days of the year when the estate is closed. The deer roam free and are a fine sight during the rutting season. My favourite time though is February when the snowdrops carpeting much of the visible ground space are a delight.

75.

76.

77.

The Skell is joined to the west of Ripon By the river Laver at Rustic Bridge. The lazy waters today belie the fact that this river has a short and steep drop with no flood plain to absorb excess water. Flash flooding from rain falling on the moors has always been a problem in Ripon but finally a holding dam is being constructed near Birkby Nab to temporarily arrest the flow.

78.

80.

As we are now in Ripon we can include the historic Market Place and its Hornblower. Now purely ceremonial it has its origins in the past when it was the duty of the Wakeman to administer justice and pay compensation if problems occurred in the city after the 9.00 p.m. curfew.

If you want the full story and a few extras besides, be on the square ANY night of the year at 9.00 p.m. and when the deed is done the story will be told.

Ripon Cathedral is another of the jewels of the area.

There has been a church on this spot for over 1300 years. The Crypt is the only remaining part from the earliest building - dated from a.d. 672. There are many fine views of the fabric of the building, this one from near Hewick Bridge over the Ure to the south east of the city. Also in view is Holy Trinity church and its fine spire, the Catholic Church of St Wilfrid to the right of the picture and the obelisk crowned with its gold horn weather vane in the distance.

81.

Whilst there is now a great religious tolerance of all denominations and regular joint services it is a standing joke that the Church of England are only looking after the Cathedral for its rightful owners the Catholic Church. But with ever spiralling maintenance costs they do not want it back! For a friendly Yorkshire welcome Ripon Cathedral has an ever open door.

82.

83.

84.

85.

86.

There are so many aspects to the city of Ripon that much has to be left out for you to discover for yourself. The motto "Stay awhile amidst its ancient charms" on the road signs coming into Ripon encourages just that.

Here I have highlighted the Ripon canal, the most northerly branch of the connected navigable waterway system and a target for boating enthusiasts. We just enjoy the peace of the towpath after the bustling city life!

The C12th Leper Chapel or Hospital Chapel of St Mary Magdalen was there to serve lepers and blind priests. The low Leper window allowed alms to be distributed.

The Ripon Museums Trust administer three important sites, the Police Museum, Workhouse and Courthouse. All are fascinating to visit and have knowledgeable and helpful staff.

The Ripon City Band have been celebrating 150 years of Brass in Ripon during 2010 Hard to miss in their bright red outfits they are often to be heard at events throughout the city.

87.

88.

89.

Ripon Racecourse holds flat meetings during spring and summer.

On leaving Ripon, the River flows past the stately grandeur of Newby Hall. Its fine herbaceous borders leading away from the banks of the Ure to a flight of steps rising to the C17th home of the Compton family.

Soon the River Ure will near its end and as it passes through Boroughbridge we can stop to admire the mysterious Devils Arrows. These are three ancient gritstone monoliths, erected by someone, sometime for some purpose. One day we may know, but how nice to have such a mystery on our doorstep.

The town of Boroughbridge has been a through route of the A1 since Roman times. Thankfully by-passed now and left to re-discover its identity, it has so far managed to retain a viable community structure with interesting shops next to quaint antiquaries.